# SMALL BUSINESS MARKETING MADE EASY

## 8 proven strategies to grow your revenue, build your reputation and create ongoing wealth

**Copyright © 2016 by Jennifer Thomé**
**All rights reserved.**

No part of this book may be reproduced or transmitted in any form or by any means, electronic or mechanical, including photocopying, recording, or by an information storage and retrieval system - except by a reviewer who may quote brief passages in a review- without permission in writing from the author.

Printed in the United State of America

First Printing: September 2016

# DEDICATION

This book is dedicated to the small business owners who work tirelessly to build a better future for themselves and their families. You take on great risk and daunting tasks to create economic opportunities and to serve your community. You make this country, and this world, great

I am grateful to the friends who have helped me both in my career as a small business owner and author. Chelsey Baker-Hauck of CBH Brand Strategy, Helene Kwong of Hashtagitude, content marketing executive Ben Tarver, and Julie Zagars, consultant extraordinaire. And of course, my dear husband Jeff, without whose delicious foods and business savvy I would never have had the chance to write this book.

# JOIN THE COMMUNITY

You can get more answers, insight and feedback from other small business owners by joining our Facebook group at **www.facebook.com/SmallBusinessMarketingMadeEasy**

# INTRODUCTION: HERE'S WHAT'S AHEAD

The mission of this book is simple: You are going to learn simple yet effective marketing strategies that will increase your bottom line without wasting your time.

Chapter 1 will teach you how to **Stock your Digital Inventory** with great photos, descriptions and videos that you can use time and time again, without searching, scrambling or editing.

Chapter 2 is all about **Creating a Brand that Sells**, both online and in person. Once you learn how to clearly express who you are and what makes your business special, you will effortlessly create sales and word of mouth buzz.

In chapter 3 you will **Develop your Digital Real Estate**—Google, Facebook, Yelp and all of the other websites where people will find your business—and you'll learn how to get found fast and how to convert those who find you into customers. This chapter will also touch upon dealing with the stinkers who will try to abuse online ratings to get their way.

Chapter 4 will help you learn to evaluate different types of advertising—print, email, social and direct mail—and **Create Effective Ads** so that you can maximize the return of every dollar you invest.

In chapter 5–**Get the Press you Deserve**–you'll discover how to get free publicity from the media, how to sell yourself without selling your soul, and how to create word-of-mouth buzz.

Chapter 6 will teach you to connect with customers by **Taking your Brand to the Streets**. This is a fun and effective way to do offline marketing. Get ready to learn where to go, what to bring, and how to sell your product in seconds.

Chapter 7 will provide guidance on how to **Grow your Digital Relationships** through social media, newsletters, forums and more.

Finally, in chapter 8, we'll talk about building meaningful relationships with other small (and big!) business owners, and how to **Weave Yourself a Profit Network** that will add revenue to your bottom line without too much additional effort.

Complete chapter 1 first, and then feel free to dive in wherever it feels right!

Remember to join our Facebook group where you can ask questions, share ideas and get more marketing freebies: **www.facebook.com/SmallBusinessMarketingMadeEasy**

# TABLE OF CONTENTS

# ABOUT THE AUTHOR

So, who am I to tell you how to market your business? Long story short, I'm a former marketer who got her butt handed to her in a takeout box when she started her own restaurant.

Back when marketing was my job, it was easy. I'd wake up late, drink lots of coffee and had eight to twelve hours a day to do *marketing*, whether that meant doing market research, developing a marketing plan, tracking results or executing campaigns.

Once we opened the restaurant it was a different story. We had to cook, clean, order supplies and take care of customers. Running the joint was more than a full time job, and marketing got stuck on the back burner. Oh, and did I mention I still had a day job and a baby? Time was of the essence!

Through hard work we were able to get our restaurant to stop bleeding money, but without marketing business was stagnant. Our concept was too unique and our location too hidden to gain real traction, and I knew that without marketing we would be going under once the slow season hit. If this was going to make this work, I had to learn to be smarter, faster, and to design marketing strategies that could generate amazing results with minimal effort.

Fast forward six months and people were lining up outside the door. After a year, we had a restaurant that was bringing in almost half a million dollars in sales, a complete turnaround for this 13-seat restaurant that had failed all of its previous owners.

We took this little place from being a tiny little dump to being the most buzzed about hole-in-the-wall in town. Our business was on fire. We had paid off our debts and started making good money. People knew us by name, they knew our story, and our hard-won customers became our advocates. Many first time visitors went out of their way to share that a friend had recommended us, the golden standard for a good business.

Later that year, we won best Chinese restaurant from the local paper and were invited to be part of a museum show featuring America's best Chinese chefs in New York. We decided to sell the business, which was still 13 little seats, but now came with a great brand, word of mouth buzz, and almost 100 4-5 star reviews.

At this point you must be thinking I am some kind of marketing genius who never sleeps, but that's far from the truth. I was exhausted and desperate, and the only advantage I had over you today is that I had experience, and that I will officially pass on to you with this book.

You, like my husband, are doing the hard work, and if you've designed a product, passed inspection and set up a business, you are more than qualified to do your own marketing.

Let me teach you how!

# STOCK YOUR MARKETING INVENTORY

*A well-stocked marketing inventory ensures that you have high-quality marketing collateral at your fingertips, making your first impressions more professional, and saving you time and hassle as you integrate marketing in your daily workflow.*

As a business owner, you get the importance of having a well-stocked, organized inventory: it allows you to quickly and effortlessly get your product into your customer's hands.

Your marketing inventory is no different. It's a storehouse of marketing images, text and videos, phrases, and things like hashtags that you can easily grab whenever you are doing your marketing. That way, you're not scrambling to get photos, wasting time searching for files, or trying to think of something clever to say when all you want to do is have a glass of wine and go to bed!

I really want to encourage you to start with this chapter because I didn't. When we started the business we were scrambling to get food on the tables and dishes washed. By the time I started marketing, my files were all over the place, and I spent days trying to retrieve them from emails, my husband, our Facebook page, etc.

That is why this chapter will teach you how to organize your files (and set up a storage infrastructure) and how to create high-quality marketing collateral that will attract customers instantly and leave a powerful first, second and third impression.

As obvious as this is, I find that most business owners struggle with creating high-quality marketing collateral, leaving their websites, Yelp pages and social media are littered with blurry images, poor copy text, and calls to action that fail to inspire action.

This is a huge problem, because it's estimated that more than 60% of people check out a business online before heading over. If your descriptions aren't descriptive enough, they may never find you. If they do happen to find you and your photos stink, they will probably choose another business.

Personally, I cannot tell you the number of times I have passed on a business because it didn't spark my interest, and the statistics prove that I am not alone.

This is why we are going to get your marketing inventory in order before doing anything else. This way, every single thing you do will seem professional, well planned, and inspire people to action.

As hard as it will be, I want you to get up early one day, close for (or after) lunch or stay up late, and spend some time do set up your inventory and create your collateral.

Trust me, if you make the time to do this right it will not only make your day-to-day marketing easier. No, it will also increase the impact your marketing has, hurrying along those increased profits you so deserve.

# ORGANIZE YOUR FILES

The first step of creating your inventory is to get organized and to set up a place where you can store your documents and make them available for quick and easy access.

This can be on a USB stick or a computer (just remember to back them up), or on the cloud, using a service like DropBox (which is what I use) or Google Drive. The benefit of being on the cloud is that you can easily share specific files or folders with staff, media or print shops, allowing you to keep all documents in one place, making sure you always have the latest copy, and sharing only those that need to be shared.

**Here's how I set up my DropBox folder:**

**Restaurant**
- *Business Operations*
    - Phone numbers, supply lists, etc.
    - Employee Info (a file on each employee, plus paystubs)
    - Accounting Files
    - Strategic Vision (business plan, goals, etc.)
- *Photos and Descriptions*
    - Dishes
        - Sample Dish.jpg
        - Complete menu with descriptions, ingredients and prices
        - Restaurant descriptions
    - Chef Photos
        - Chef Bio.doc
        - Chef Photo.jpg
    - Travel Photos
    - Customer/Shop Photos
- *Printing (Menus, posters, etc.)*
    - Word doc with printer information (local print shop, online orders, etc.)
    - Menu.doc
    - Menu.jpg or .pdf
    - Poster.doc
    - Poster.jpg or .pdf
- *Marketing and Advertising*
    - Advertising Files
    - Advertising and Media Contacts (Spreadsheet or Document)
    - Sound bytes and Statements

# CREATING GREAT PRODUCT PHOTOS

You know how they call it food porn?

It's not because the bananas are peeling themselves provocatively, but because like actual pornography, great photos tap deep into our animal instincts, causing our brain to say: "That looks amazing! I must have it NOW!"

When we opened our restaurant I got many offers from photographers promising to take great photos for the "small" sum of $600-2,000. That's a lot of money for a small business! If you can afford it: GREAT. If not, read on to learn how to take great photos.

80% of our photos were taken with a newer iPhone, which has an amazing camera that shoots pictures fit for print.

For the restaurant, we threw a party and invited all of our friends to sample the food. We took the photos (as did they!) as the food came out of the kitchen, and by the end of the day we had a ton of photos and a handful of reviews from people who loved the food. We also got some photos of the restaurant brimming with people, which was great for marketing.

**Step One: Prepare your Product**
Make sure your product is well presented. Polish, iron, style your product until it looks gorgeous. For food, you generally want to undercook it a little, and brush or spray it with oil to make it glisten. Make sure to clean up any drop or smudges. For merchandise, you want to make sure it's clean, straight, and that you have a neutral background to put it on.

**Step Two: Adjust your Lighting**
Ideally, you should only have one source of light to avoid discoloration. Check to see if your light is creating shadows behind your product. Make sure that you can't see your reflection or your shadow in the photo.

**Step Three: Shoot from the Right Angle**
Play around with a few angles to find the one that suits your product best. Your product should take anywhere between 50-80% of the space of the photo. Shoot a few different angles to create a variety of materials.

**Step Four: Edit your Photo**
It's hard to shoot the perfect photo, but you can use simple tools like adjusting the lighting, correcting a spot, or cropping the photo to make it look great.

*TIP! Go on Pinterest and search for photos of what you're selling. You'll be able to find some great examples of what your product photos should look like.*

# CREATING GREAT PRODUCT DESCRIPTIONS

Photo are crucial for hooking your customer and getting them excited, but they won't find you unless your words and phrases are clear and searchable.

This is called Search Engine Optimization (SEO), which is really a fancy way of saying that you phrase things the way your audience would phrase them, using as many keywords as possible. That way, when they search for you, you'll actually appear!

**Many business owners are either too terse or too elaborate in their writing, and both end up with the same results: bad business.**

If your descriptions are too terse, you may miss some phrase or keyword the customer is looking for.

If you use words that are too elaborate or floral, or sentence structures that are too convoluted, you may lose business because that is also not what people are typing into the search bar.

*Here's an example: Xiao Long Bao*

"Xiao Long Bao? What's that?" We were asked this question a million times at the restaurant, even though it was one of our most popular items. People in the know knew that it was soup dumplings, but many could not remember that name. If we had written it like that in our Yelp description, they would never have found us, because they were likely searching for "soup dumplings" or "dim sum." So, the perfect description for Xiao Long Bao is: Xiao Long Bao Soup Dumplings, a Dim Sum favorite.

# THE FIVE PARTS OF GREAT PRODUCT DESCRIPTIONS

A great product description allows the customer to find what they are looking for, and then brings the product to life before their eyes.

**Here are the five parts of a great product description:**

**Fully State What You Do**
Simple, right? Yet 70% of online profiles don't do this. Start with the type of business you are, followed the services and products you offer and how they can be used.

**List Everything You Offer**
This way, people looking for specific things will be able to find you. I am always looking for Turkish coffee, but Middle Eastern grocery stores never list this. If I didn't know to dig deeper, I would have to order it online.

**Don't Be Too Frilly**
When you say too much, your reader may become overwhelmed or bored. When you use big words that don't come natural to the customer, their common language search results will not be directed to your listing.

**Use Logical Word Order**
Write things the way that your audience would write them. Don't be overly technical. If in doubt, run it past someone who is not in your line of work.

**Mention The Things You Don't Have (but can provide an alternative to)**
You're probably thinking: Why on earth would you highlight the fact that you don't offer something? You do it because people might be looking for that product, but you offer a great alternative. This is especially effective if you are offering a more reasonable and affordable alternative to something.

# PRODUCT DESCRIPTION EXAMPLE

My guess is only a few of you know what Thermage is, meaning that if you needed it, you probably wouldn't search for it by that name. So let's use this as an example to talk about how to write great product descriptions.

Thermage is an anti-aging treatment that uses radio frequency technology to increase collagen production. Bam! It's a marvel of modern science and one of the secrets to Gwyneth Paltrow's gorgeous complexion.

The only problem with it is that its name tells us nothing about it. Here's how we would remedy this problem if it were our product:

**Part 1: Fully State What You Do**
Now, if I was looking for an anti-aging facial, I may or may not find your spa because you didn't use the phrase "anti-aging facial." If someone else did, they would pop up first. This is what I mean when I say complete descriptions. You should have all the key words related to your products or services in your listing, and if you are location specific, mention that, too! Perhaps someone is searching for "best anti-aging facial in [your city]."

**Part 2: List Everything You Offer**
One you've written a thorough description, you'll want to make sure you list everything that you offer. For a spa, it might be other services (manicures, pedicures, toenail fungus laser, IPL spot removal, etc.).

**Part 3: Don't Be Too Frilly**
You don't have to explain the science of how the procedure works in detail. Most customers aren't searching for words like "dermis" or "collagen." Make sure that what you're writing reflects the things that people are trying to find. You can always wow them with your expert knowledge once they walk through the door.

**Part 4: Use Logical Word Order**
If you say: our facial has anti-aging capabilities, people searching for anti-aging facial might be led elsewhere. If you say "we have food from China" people who are looking for "Chinese food" will end up with the competition.

**Part 5: State What You Don't Have**
Thermage is actually a great alternative to a facelift, so mention that! Your customer may be looking for a facelift, and you can save them thousands of dollars and provide them with great results, all with zero downtime.

# CREATE A BRAND THAT SELLS

*A good brand creates customer loyalty, allows you to charge higher prices for your good and services, facilitates word of mouth and viral marketing, and will earn you a higher price on your stocks and your business should you choose to sell it.*

No matter what your business is, having a good brand is essential. It allows your customers to find you, to fall in love with you, and to talk about you to their friends and family. It also helps you to easily and quickly articulate why your product is better than anyone else's.

Take Nike or Apple. I am certain they spend more money on promoting themselves than they do on manufacturing. Why? Because when they do, the mere mention or memory of their brand sparks a rush of feelings that makes people want to buy more of their things.

I'm sure that there are many other shoes that are as good as Nike's, but none makes the customer feel more empowered. And 800 dollars for a phone is ridiculous, but I gladly pay it because Apple makes everything so smooth and easy.

So let's take a moment to talk about the elements of a great brand.

You need a good name, striking visuals, a company promise that invokes feelings in the customers and a great story.

If you already have a brand: awesome! Skip the next section and we'll talk about how to refine and distill it. If you're new to owning your own business, then the next chapter is for you.

*In short, a great brand is a direct pipeline to ongoing and increasing sales.*

# BUILDING A BRAND FROM SCRATCH

If you're building a brand from scratch, I strongly encourage you to take a moment to think about the audience that you are going to serve and what their needs and likes are.

So many business owners make one simple mistake: they create a product they love and assume the world will fall in love with it, too. We assume that everyone shares our tastes, but if that were the case, why hasn't someone else created your very product? Think about this!

Once you've come to terms with this ground shattering reality the real fun begins. Take a few minutes to answer the following questions as thoroughly as possible:

**What exactly am I selling?**
Describe the product AND the feeling you want it to invoke in people.

**Who is going to give me money for this?**
Describe your customers or clients as best as you can. Who are they? What do they do? How do they like to shop, and most importantly, what problem are you fixing for them?

**What other types of products are they going to buy?**
If you could peep into their trunks after a day of shopping, what would you find there? If they were running short on time, what would prompt them to come to your shop instead of someone else's?

**Why would they choose my product above the competition?**
Do you offer a better value? Are you flashier? More delicious or healthy? Write down the name of your competition and then three reasons why you offer a better product for your customer. Also write down some reasons why they would choose you over not spending their time and money.

**Why do they want to buy it from me?**
Do you have a unique story? Do you support a good cause? Is there any kind of human connection between you and your customer?

**Why am I doing this business?**
Seriously? Why are you doing this? To support your family or because you are an inspired genius? The *Why* is an important part of your story, not to mention, your anchor in rough times.

**Where and how are they going to purchase my product?**
How will they find you? How do they want their product delivered to them?

*Once you're done with this exercise, print the answers and post them on your wall. This is as much a dream board as a reminder to keep you grounded. It is also a roadmap to your success.*

# HOW WE DESIGNED THE FLOWER PEPPER BRAND

Let me share a little of my story to help you understand how this works: When we started thinking about a restaurant I wanted to do something amazing. Local, Organic produce AND authentic Chinese food. I was going to call it Chi-Lo. Chinese Local. To me, this seemed like the perfect brand, but luckily I asked my friends and they told me that it was a flop.

***It turns out, I had committed the #1 branding mistake, which is assuming that I have better taste than my customers.***

Our location was located on the fringe of a hospital complex. Our customers–medical and office staff–didn't care about organic, and they didn't necessarily care about authentic, although that was definitely something that sparked their interest. They wanted clean, fast and tasty.

We also had to compete with chain restaurants and coffee shops nearby, meaning that price was a deciding factor, and organic food was not a viable option.

So we designed our menu to be filling and delicious, but more importantly: fast. American Chinese food is known for being greasy and heavy, so we chose a name that set us apart: Flower Pepper Restaurant.

It was named after China's most unique ingredient: the Flower (or Sichuan) Pepper. It was unique enough to separate us from regular Chinese restaurants that use words like Mandarin, Peking, Szechuan, etc.

When we first started, we tried using words like "Authentic Chinese Fast Food" to describe ourselves, but when Americans think fast food they think fried food, so the healthier customers didn't want to buy it, and the fat-loving foodies were disappointed. Home Cooking seemed to be a good fit. We eventually decided on "Flower Pepper: Authentic Chinese Home Cooking."

To further set ourselves apart, we decided to do our marketing materials in the Gotham font, the same font used by the Obama campaign. It was bold, clean and powerful. We then added elements in the Bonzai font, which is very Asian. The message we sent was clear: We are clean, fast, fun, but we serve amazing Chinese food.

For our logo, we decided to use a digital rendering of the actual Flower Pepper. Unique and modern, but approachable, and not too Chinese-y, despite the fact that we were more Chinese than any other shop in town.

# THE ELEMENTS OF A GREAT BRAND

The most important thing a brand can do is to evoke a primal emotion that makes your customer want to buy your product.

**There are four elements of a great brand, known as The Four P's: Purpose, Positioning, Promise and Personality.**

**Purpose:** The mission of your company. Why are you in this business? Is it to be your own boss? Is it because you are passionate about the cause? Is it because you love serving people? Take a minute to articulate your purpose, as that will be the opening to your brand story.

Our purpose was to make a living, but also to bring authentic Chinese food to Boulder. Knowing this, we focused on sharing our experiences in China, explaining the dishes and their origin, and hung pictures from our travels to remote areas.

**Positioning:** Where do you stand in the market? Are you a high-end brand or an everyday brand? Do you serve women or men, singles or families? Are you practical or a luxury? Toilet paper aside there are few brands that are designed for everyone, so get clear on your positioning, because that will dictate who you tell your story to, and how you style your brand.

Take, for example, Android versus Apple. Both are smart phones and they pretty much do the same darn thing, yet people treat them like they are different religions. Here's an interesting fact: brain scans have revealed that brand loyalty activates the same parts of the brain as religious faith. Android is young and hip, independent. Apple is smart, elegant, and bold.

**Personality:** If your brand was a person, what would they be like? Bold or Beautiful? Funny or Serious? Wise or a wiseass? This will dictate how you interact with the people that you come into contact with, and the voice of your marketing efforts.

Our brand was straightforward. Simple food, no fuss, and a passion for all things Chinese. On our social media we shared recipes, news articles and gorgeous videos, and when talking to customers we treated them like we would our friends.

**Promise:** What will the customer get in exchange for their money? A luxurious experience with great customer service, or the best damn meal of their life without any frills?

I always felt bad that we couldn't offer a more comfortable eat-in experience, but once I decided that great food was my promise, it became easy to focus on that and I discovered that 99% of our customers didn't care about the space limitations.

# BRANDING CHECKLIST

Here is a checklist of Either-Ors that can help you narrow down your brand's identity. It's ok to check both or none, as this is a tool to help you articulate what you want your brand to feel like.

| THIS | OR | THAT |
|---|---|---|
| New | | Established |
| Hip | | Wise |
| Expensive | | Cheap |
| Luxurious | | Comfortable |
| Funny | | Serious |
| Everyday | | Special Occasion |
| For Women | | For Men |
| For Families | | For Singles |
| For Locals | | For Visitors |
| Exotic | | Familiar |
| Expert Advice | | Open to All |
| Community | | Individual |
| Fast | | Slow |
| Self Service | | Full Service |
| Big | | Small |
| Colorful and Fun | | Sophisticated |
| Great Customer Service | | Great Prices |
| Masculine | | Feminine |
| Prestigious | | Comfortable |
| High Tech | | Low Tech |
| Urban | | Rural |
| Local | | International |
| Beethoven | | Beyoncé |
| Kids | | Teenagers |
| Young People | | Adults |
| Adults | | Grandparents |
| Stylish | | Comfortable |
| All-American | | Exotic |
| | | |
| | | |
| | | |
| | | |
| | | |
| | | |

# BRAND PLANNER

Below is a simple brand planner that you can use to brainstorm your brand. Once you've come up with a few ideas, invite some friends who would make great customers for drinks, and ask them what they think. Be prepared for honest feedback, and to take all feedback with a grain of salt. After the first meeting, you can either schedule a follow up, or do an email or Facebook chat to refine your ideas.

One of the extra benefits of doing this is that you're already building brand ambassadors, so once you launch, you'll have a team excited to help you spread the word!

| We are going to sell: |
| --- |
| |

| We are going to sell it to: |
| --- |
| |

| Our competition is _____, and this is why we are better: |
| --- |
| |

| We're thinking of calling it: |
| --- |
| |

| If you saw this, would you buy it? Why or why not? |
| --- |
| |

| Any other thoughts? |
| --- |
| |

# WRITING YOUR ELEVATOR PITCH & BRAND STORY

The average person's attention span is now on par with that of a fish. Thank you social media!

The great news about this is that we are very distractible, so if you can grab someone's attention, they are, for one brief moment in time, all yours.

The formula for an elevator pitch is simple: We do [your product plus descriptor] for [this kind of person] in order to [what does your product solve or provide?].

**Here are some examples of straightforward elevator pitches:**

Flower Pepper Restaurant serves authentic Chinese home cooking to people who are sick of Americanized Chinese food.
My beauty company sells organic products that help people stay young without the chemicals.
My tech company provides software that helps parents connect with other parents, people to organize their finances, allows young people feel more empowered... etc.

**The elevator pitch is your hook, and then you follow it up with a clear brand story.**

I am so and so, and I discovered that there was a need for this product (either in the market or for myself). Here is how I built this company, and here is how people have felt about it.

**Here is ours – with notes in red italics to help you understand why I added things**

Jeff Gao is an award-winning restaurateur *Why he's qualified to serve you*
Who fell in love with Colorado and moved there *Why he chose this area – creating connection*
He was crushed to discover that there was no good Chinese food in this area, only American Chinese food, which is way too heavy, sticky and sweet *Explain the market need, push down the competition*
so he decided to roll up his sleeves and start an authentic Chinese restaurant, serving "fresh, home cooked" meals. *Here's what we do in a nutshell*
It was a struggle and he invested every penny he had, *People love supporting the underdog*
but thanks to the support of the community, *You love us! Social validation for the win!*
business is finally taking off. *And we're a success!*
It's not for everyone, but the people who are sick of greasy brown sauce have loved our fresh noodles and dumplings. *Awesome people like you love us and losers don't, so that's why we have a few bad reviews.*

# Stuck? Try Answering the WHY's

If you're still having trouble writing and telling your brand story, start by answering these WHY questions. Once you do, you can build a brand even your harshest critic will get, even if that person is you.

**Why is your product/shop around?**
Did you see a need for this product? A gap in the market? An opportunity to provide better quality or service? Any of these reasons is a good one.

**Why do you do this kind of work?**
Do you want to serve the community? Provide people with amazing experiences? Make enough money so that you can take care of your family or pay off your debts?

**Why should people give you their money?**
Does your product make them feel good? Help them lead a better life? Does it help them solve a problem or fill a need? Fill their tummies or nurture their bodies?

**Why should your customers tell their friends about your business?**
Because they like you? Because they respect you? Because you gave them a great experience and quality service?

If you can answer these questions, you will not only recognize your worth (which is priceless on the bad days) but also build a solid foundation for your story.

**When the WHY isn't working**

Sometimes you may find that the why isn't working, and this should be a red flag to sit down, take a deep breath, and really think about your business and your mission.

At the end of the day, every business needs to make money, but if your why is "I just want to make money by all means necessary" then chances are this attitude is showing in your story, your work, and your relationship with your customers.

Always remember that business is one big transaction. You invest your time and your money to create a great business, and that is incredibly hard and packed with uncertainty. It's easy to think yourself more deserving than the customer, especially when they are ungrateful of your hard work, but remember that they also traded in their time and their labor for the money they are giving you.

All of us are dealing in time, energy and money, but in this situation, you have the power to provide them with a truly great experience.

# HOW TO DESIGN A LOGO

Having a logo isn't everything, but it does help activate the visual centers of your brain in a way that words and ideas can't. That's why you should invest some time and a little bit of money to make it a good one.

Now, if you're anything like me, visuals aren't your thing. If that is the case, I suggest heading over to Shutterstock.com and searching for "your business" logo. In most cases, you'll be instantly overwhelmed with how many images there are, and thrilled to find out that most of them can be purchased for commercial use for under 30 dollars. If you can find something you love here, I suggest going for it. Why? Because designing a logo is an expensive pain in the butt and a distraction from doing business. So many people get wrapped up in planning their business when they should be focusing on execution.

**Some things you'll want to keep in mind before you buy a logo are:**

- Does it match the feel of my company?
- Does the color match my products or resonate with the company?
- Is the competition using something similar? Is it unique enough?
- Could it be mistaken for something else? Does it make sense for my company?
- Is it catchy?
- Is it simple enough to stick in people's minds?

Collect a couple of ideas and run this past your friends and acquaintances. People love sharing feedback, especially if it's over coffee, dinner or ice cream.

**True Story**

Here's a true story that I think will make you snicker: I spent a weeks coming up with my company's name: PraMaSo, which stands for Practical Marketing Solutions. It was clever, modern, easy to pronounce, and it looked great in my favorite font. Then I went to design a logo and I was stumped. What represents a marketing company? I decided to go for initials... which happens to be PMS! Oh well! You live, you learn.

**Getting a Logo Designed**

For those of you who have a great artistic vision and know what you want, designing a logo is an option. If you're designing something simple and you are very good at articulating what you want, you can get a steal at sites like Fiverr.com, though I will say my experience with them has been hit or miss. You can also turn to sites like Odesk.com, and even your local university's student media department to have something designed for anywhere between 50-200 dollars. A professional designer will run you anywhere between 500-2,000 dollars, and will agree to revisions and should provide you with a good amount of branding collateral and a brand guide.

# TRAINING YOUR STAFF IN YOUR BRAND

Hiring and training staff is hard. It's not their company, and they are (hopefully!) making less money than you, so why should they care as much as you do?

That's where great branding can help! By creating a great brand and sharing it with them you can create loyalty and buy-in from your staff, and they in turn, will get the same from your customers.

### 1. Share your Story
Make sure that every employee knows your brand story. It's something to latch on to, and it gives them a clear understanding of you and the company. When a customer asks, they will be able to share that with them.

### 2. Share your Brand
When my brother came to work for us, he was so excited about introducing new dishes, doing some fusion cooking and being a great chef... it broke my heart to have to stop him. I loved his passion, but it was not in line with our brand, and the customers found it confusing.

### 3. Share your Vision
What are you aspiring to? If you are an employee, chances are it is to have a cushy job that will grow your career and hopefully not be littered with a-holes. If, however, you have an inspiring boss who is going to do something for the greater good (even if that is providing cupcakes that make people happy!), then you aspire to make them happy and do great things.

### 4. Share your Values
Core values can bind people together in a very powerful way. Is your mission to be helpful? To be fun? To be fabulous? Share this with your staff, and reward them when they act in line with your values. You may have some people drop out because they don't want to be bubbly and outgoing, and that's ok: they are making room for better staff.

### 5. Set Clear Expectations
Most employees get frustrated because they aren't given clear directions or feedback and they feel uncertain about whether or not they are doing the right thing. To prevent that bad energy from ever happening, grab a coffee with them on day one and regularly thereafter so that they are always aware of how they are doing.

### 6. Treat them as your would your Customers
By treating your staff the way you would treat your customers, you are setting the bar on customer service. Remember, both are financial transactions: Your customers are paying you for an experience, and you are paying your staff to provide it.

# BRANDING IN ACTION

When your customer asks for a recommendation, give them a story! Here's one of mine:

I really love *Zhajiang* noodles. I remember the first time I had them like it was yesterday. My future husband took me to an old restaurant near the Forbidden City. It was so noisy and full of life. The waiter brought me this giant bowl of noodles with a bowl thick, luscious sauce, and a stack of tiny plates a foot high. In them were shredded carrots, cucumbers, purple radishes, and more. It was so precarious. So noisy. We mixed everything and it made the most satisfying dish I've ever had.

This is a true story, and boy does it sells noodles. I also have a story for every other dish. That is branding in action!

**Here are some great ways to use your branding every single day:**

### Tell a Story
Telling stories create instant connections. It may be your story or someone else's, but when you take the time to share it not only does it bring your product to life, it also creates a real human connection, which is priceless.

### Wear your Work Clothes or a Signature Items
Got a cool brand? Why not show it off while you're running errands. My signature style is wearing Chinese earrings. People ask me where I got them while we are standing in line, and I share that I picked them up while we were researching rice noodles in Guilin, etc.

### Share your Stories on Social Media
Sharing your business stuff on your social media may seem questionable, but sharing stories is what social media was actually designed to do! Crappy customers, the day the shop flooded, the fact that you sold out... You'd be surprised how many of your connections missed that you started a business and will chime in to cheer you on.

### Offer Advice
When you hear someone talking about something you know about, feel free to chime in. It catches people off guard, but people tend to be impressed that I pay attention to my customers. Even if you're out and about, you can easily garner new business by sharing your expertise by sharing a story like this: "I run a small noodle shop in Boulder, and I once had the worst customer/a busted water heater/was so tired/had to find an accountant... and here's what I learned."

### Question: isn't this a little tacky?
The answer is NO! Forcing someone to listen to your sales pitch is tacky, but offering to share insight, expertise and experience related to your work is not. Your business is an important part of your life, and it would be silly not to talk about it.

# DEVELOP YOUR DIGITAL REAL ESTATE

*Your business success rests not only on your physical location, but your digital location. It is essential to create online listings that allow your customers to find you and your products.*

They say that opening a business is all about location, and even if your business is an online one, that has never been more true. If people can't find you, they can't buy from you. That is why you have to develop your digital real estate.

In this day and age, people tend to either do their shopping online, or pop onto the internet to find things they want to go pick up in person. Depending on your category, close to 60% of sales are started through a search engine like Google, a review website like Yelp, third party sellers website like Groupon, Amazon or Etsy or online delivery services.

By creating accurate, descriptive and popular profiles in these digital locales, you can ensure that you will be the first company anyone finds when they are looking for your product online.

Back when we opened the restaurant, I spent a good amount of time optimizing our Yelp page, and it really paid off. We quickly went from 2-3 customers and hour to a steady flow of customers every day. By the time we sold the restaurant, we were getting 2,000 views a month on Yelp, 500 of which would click through to order online, get directions or call us.

*We got most of our customers by investing a little time in our online profiles, making it our biggest sales channel next to word of mouth.*

We also got a ton of attention from listing our restaurant on various other websites, such as food delivery sites. This way, we didn't have to pay for surprisingly expensive advertising in the college paper, and instead, enjoyed a good amount of business from a 3$^{rd}$ party app, who took about 25% of profits – still less than we would have paid for advertising, and plus, we didn't have to hire a driver.

Now, you may be looking for someone to hold your hand and walk you through every step of the process. I would love to do that in this book, but these website are forever changing, so anything I teach you would likely be out of date before this book hits the press.

Instead, I started a Facebook group where you can ask questions, share feedback, and meet other small business owners. You can find us at: **www.facebook.com/SmallBusinessMarketingMadeEasy**

# ACTIVE VS. PASSIVE MARKETING

Many small business want to start with the fun stuff, such as social media and advertising. Bad move!

While these things do have an impact and can bring in more customers, they are active marketing strategies – something you have to be engaged with and maintain on a day-to-day basis in order for it to pay off. These require time, energy and content, and in the early growth stages of a business those tend to be in short supply.

But even more importantly, if you haven't set up your passive marketing channels a lot of your efforts will be going straight down the drain.

Passive marketing – such as good profiles online – is something that you build and it does the work for you even when you don't have time or energy, which makes it perfect for a busy small business owner.

When you start by setting up your passive marketing channels, the active marketing that you do will have a much greater impact in the long run: people who see your post on social media check our your profile and see how awesome you are, or search for you on Google or Yelp see tons of great photos as well as some good reviews.

Think of it as setting up a foundation to build your business on: the better of a job you do creating an enticing place for people to gather, the more likely they are to come and to come back.

You wouldn't skip on paining and decorating your shop, so why wouldn't you take the time to make sure that the 70% of customers who will check our your business online and on social media won't be able to resist visiting your online shop or your physical location.

# How to Choose your Location

Choosing the location of your digital real estate is one of the most important decisions you'll make for your business. It can create passive income, make you instantly available to people searching for you, and gives your most loyal customers the chance to write you stellar reviews.

That all being said, you want to make sure to choose your locations wisely, because each property needs to be maintained in order to be effective. It's tempting to sign up everywhere, but it's better to do a good job on a few sites than to scare people away with a lot of poorly maintained sites.

Here are the top three things you should look for when choosing your digital real estate locations:

**Suitability**
Ask yourself: Does this particular attract the kinds of people you are looking for?
Sometimes I see items selling for a couple thousand on Amazon.com and I can't help but wonder: "What were you thinking?!" I would never buy something that expensive unless I knew it came from a trusted seller, and certainly not before checking it out in person.

**Reach**
Now, the next thing you need to consider is reach. Does this website attract enough customers to eventually convert some of them into your customers? This is where sites like Amazon.com and Overstock.com are great. They bring in millions of customers every day, meaning that if you develop your real estate properly, you might be able to score big with these sites.

There are some niche sites that may be great for your product, but be sure to ask them about their hits (how many people visit their site) and their conversion rate (how many people buy things from their site). You can also ask them about their bounce rate (how many people leave the site without doing anything) and the average time spent on their site by customers.

In our case, we signed up for a number of delivery sites, on top of places like Yelp.com and AllMenu.com. We didn't have enough delivery business to warrant our own driver, but these websites also provided great advertising. Anyone who used them to order Chinese food saw our listing, meaning we didn't have to spend money advertising in those areas.

**Competition**
We all know that a little competition is good for business: it keeps us honest and pushes us to take a look at our business, decide what is and isn't working, and to evolve. That being said, the competition can also suck, force us to undervalue our products, and even write fake reviews to try to steal our business.

That is why it's critical to look at the competition when choosing your online platform. For restaurants and brick and mortar businesses, you definitely want to be on Yelp.com and Google Maps. But for people selling products in the digital space you'll want to make sure that there aren't too many people doing the same thing or doing it very cheaply, unless of course, they are doing a terrible job.

If you run into a situation when the competition is just rocking it that doesn't mean you can't do it, only that you will have to invest more time and money doing it.

# 5 STEPS TO DEVELOP YOUR DIGITAL REAL ESTATE

## 1. Choose the Right Location

Local businesses should be on Yelp, Google, YP.com, etc. Companies can benefit greatly from 3$^{rd}$ party services because these companies already have a ton of traffic going to them. No need to build your own following when you can piggyback on theirs!

Other businesses may be less intuitive, but you can quickly discover where you should be by searching for your type of business, and if you're a local, your location. See where your competition is and then hop on with a better profile!

If you're setting up a website, you can submit the URL to various search engines directly, or do a search for "Search Engine Submission" and use a third party service that will do it for you.

## 2. Describe your Product Fully

Remember when we spent all that time writing product descriptions? Now it's time to use them again! Be sure to include everything that your customer may be searching for—whether it's "Chinese food" or the name of a specific dish, a certain type of repair or beauty treatment—and to include critical key words people care about, like "organic" and "child-friendly."

*Tip: Be sure to include the general category, like "Chinese food" or "car repair" – I have seen so many businesses that don't show up in search results because they forgot to mention what they do.*

## 3. List everything that you offer

It's important to describe your company well, and it's equally important to list everything that you offer. Some people are looking for very specific things and they won't find you if you fail to mention them.

Here's a great example of how this works: I once had a woman butcher my hair, and needed a color correction. I couldn't find anyone local, so I contacted a hairdresser who was known for being good with color and asked her to help. She did an amazing job! When I wrote her review I specifically mentioned "color correction" and her business shot through the roof. Apparently it's a major concern, but because she wasn't advertising that service she never got that business. The next time I tried to book her there was a month's waiting list, but luckily she remembered me and squeezed me in.

## 4. Add great photos

Photos activate the deepest, most primitive and impulsive parts of our brain. Not only that, but photos can also save you a lot of trouble by helping customers answer their own questions. Is this place romantic? Does this product fit with my design scheme? A picture is worth a thousand words.

Remember to always label and caption your photos. That way even your photos will show up in searches.

## 5. Treat your customers with respect

Being popular online has a lot of perks, but it also creates a big vulnerability: you are now open for public discussion and review, and people who find businesses online often like to review them online.

We will talk about reputation management later, but for now, be sure to provide customers with a great experience, even when you don't feel like offering one.

# How to get More Reviews

Reviews can really make a business. Did you know that more than 60% of customers will read the reviews before heading to an establishment or making a purchase?

When you're first starting out, it can seem tempting to jump in and do a bunch of advertising, but I always advise clients to get some good reviews first. Why? Because if you drive people to your Yelp listing or sales page and there are no reviews, they are far less likely to spend their money with you because you don't have social validation.

What's more, many websites have built-in algorithms that drive more traffic to a product or listing if it already has reviews. This can also give you an edge when people aren't looking for your business, but are searching for you product.

**Here are some ways you can get reviews:**

**Ask your friends and family**
Invite your network to sample your product. Send them free copies. Invite them for an exclusive dinner. Share your story with them. And then, ask them if they can you a review, maybe even share it on more than one platform. Be sure to make it easy for them by sending a link along with your request.

**Print review cards**
Print out some postcards or business cards that ask people to leave a review. Always include the website of your choice and a link or QR code (if your audience is younger). Initially we did a few small posters around the restaurant, but decided cards were easier. We could give them to customers who loved us, and hide them from the people who gave us bad vibes.

**Offer a reward**
As a small business owner you don't have money to throw around, but you do have margins. Now, if your product costs is 30%, then why not offer people 25% off their next visit? You're still making 45%, and for the time they spent on your review, you get more business at full price.

# How to Deal with a Bad Review

The great thing about digital real estate is that it's public, mostly free, and a great way to drive business to your business. The bad thing about it is that any jerk can go and leave a negative review.

Branding is about feelings, and nothing is more important when dealing with your customers. Based on ten years worth of experience, the reason 90% of people leave reviews is because you either made them feel awesome or like crap.

The other 10% tend to be people who write about businesses because they like the attention, love writing, or like giving feedback.

In a perfect world, you and your staff would always have enough time, energy and interest to give everyone a 5-star experience, but sometimes it just doesn't happen. A table doesn't get cleaned, someone is having a bad day... try as you will, chances are you will eventually get a bad review.

The best way to deal with this is to reach out to the customer directly (sometimes you can get their info from the order, sometimes you have to do it through the site where they rated you) and tell them that this is not how you run your business, that you're sorry, and that you would like to refund them or invite them to try it again, on the house.

**For me, these kids of apologies usually went as follows:**

Dear So-and-So,
Thank you for taking the time to share your experience. I'm sorry to hear that we did not live up to your standards (be specific). We just hired new staff and they might not have been trained well enough yet (or whatever your excuse is, and you can always explain what you've done to remedy it). I personally hate spending money on things that don't live up to my expectations, and I am happy to refund you or have you back for another dinner on the house. You can reach me (I would leave my personal number) to set it up.

In most cases, I got one more star or a second chance, and in the few cases that I didn't, I would re-post the comment publicly so that people know that the owner is engaged and cares.

According to Conversocial, "88% of consumers are less likely to buy from companies who leave complaints unattended" and a 2011 Harris poll found that 33% of customers who got a prompt response to their negative review turned around and posted a positive one, and 34% deleted the original one.

People respect and appreciate honesty, and they are also considerate when you explain that you are a small business. I once had someone give us a bad review because they thought we were a chain restaurant, but when I explained that we are mom and pop, they immediately changed their opinion.

Even more surprisingly, I once had a woman offer to be my spy after leaving a mediocre review that I quickly dealt with. Our seasoned manager had been rude to her, but when I explained that he's grumpy because he'd sold his own restaurant and hated working for others, she insisted on spying on him and doing it on her own dime.

# HOW TO DEAL WITH AN AWFUL CUSTOMER

Sometimes you get people who are trying to take advantage of the system or trying to make themselves feel better. We have had customers claim to get sick when they took one bite, didn't like it, and left. We were a small place so this was easy to monitor.

In one instance, a family had ordered about 8 different dishes, and we could tell they just didn't like it. They barely touched it and left without eating anything. They were probably expecting American Chinese food. The next day they wrote saying *everyone* got *really* sick. They didn't know how it was possible, and it wasn't, since our friends, our regulars and we ourselves had all eaten the same things and were fine. It was clear that they were just trying to get their money back.

In these cases, I *always* choose compassion.

It happens: They order something they didn't like, and it leaves them with a bitter taste. The cost to me is far less than the cost to my customer, unless they write a bad review. Then my loss is exponential.

I told them that I investigated it, asked other customers and that I could not find the cause of their illness. I also mentioned that we saw that they didn't like their food and we know that happens when you're serving authentic food, so we're happy to offer them a refund. He was very happy to hear it, and admitted it *might* have been something else.

Some people also just want to take out their bad moods on you because you're an easy target and they are having a shitty day/life. It's happened to me before, and it was terrifying. In retrospect, my husband said we should have refused her service because if they don't eat the food and leave a bad review you can have it deleted. But we didn't think of it at that time and got a one start review. Here's what happened:

A lady came into the restaurant with her husband and child. They ordered food at the counter, the husband paid and left a small tip, and they sat down. A few moments she came back, seething, and asked us for the tip back. I told her sure. She was immediately embarrassed and demanded to know if other people tipped. I told her yes. Not all, but many did. She went on the defensive, saying the place is small. I explained that we serve the food and clean up after customers, and that about 50-75% of our customers tip. We even showed her the record on our POS, at which she flew into a blind rage, accusing us of making her sound like a country bumpkin who didn't know how tipping works. It went downhill from there, and two weeks later she wrote a terrible 1-star review.

At the time, I was angry and scared. We had worked so hard to set up a business, and this woman was determined to make us look bad. In some cases you can reason with people, but we knew she was a hopeless case, so I wrote to Yelp.com and Google.com and asked them to remove the reviews (one did, one didn't) and I simply left a public comment politely stating my side of the story.

A few months later, we had so many good reviews that hers didn't even make a ding in our reputation, and now, when I read her ridiculous review, I can't help but smile and celebrate how far we've come.

# How to Deal with a Fake Review

We got a handful of reviews where the food was described as bland (which it's never, unless you forgot your tongue at home) followed by a glowing endorsement for the competition. I was able to get most of these removed by Yelp because they were likely written by someone affiliated with the competition.

Whenever these kinds of reviews popped up I would snoop out the person, read their other reviews, and if I suspected they were affiliated with the competition, I would send an email to customer support at that website. Sometimes they removed it, sometimes they didn't. All you can do is build a good case against them (it has to make them look like a fraud) and hope for the best.

If the reviews weren't removed, I would follow standard protocol: I'd reach out to the customer and offer them a reimbursement or a new meal via private message. If that didn't work, I'd leave a public comment saying that I'm sorry they had a bad experience, that this doesn't sound like our business/that we're sorry to have disappointed, and that they can come ask for us if they'd like a refund.

Now, I will add here that many people believe you can get a bad review removed if you are an advertiser. You can try, but I have never seen this happen, despite the fact that I was a paying advertiser.

When you get your first bad review it seems like the world is going to come to an end, but it won't. Sometimes they are great wake up call and sometimes they are bad luck, but ultimately, each comment allows you to reassert your position as an awesome small business owner and to refine your brand.

After a while, your good buzz will be so solid that when a whackadoodle does leave a bad review, it will seem like a pebble in your shoe or a joke. Do your best to provide great service, to make things right, and to ensure that every following customer has no reason to leave you anything but a 4+ star review.

At Flower Pepper we had our ups and downs, but when we left we had close to 100 reviews averaging 4.5 stars, and a loyal word-of-mouth following. Sometimes we had customers come in and say: "Did you read that crazy review? They were clearly working for the competition or high!"

# DO I NEED MY OWN WEBSITE?

I often get asked whether or not people should set up their own website. Well, it depends.

A website can be a great place to share your story, but if you are brick and mortar or running a web business on another site, it can be a lot of extra maintenance. If you decide to do one, you'll want to do it right, and so you have to ask yourself if you have time to do a website and if it will help you sell more products.

For most small businesses and brands, I suggest creating a simple website that has your story, a list of products with descriptions, some great pictures and contact information. Put a link on your digital real estate profiles and let it do its own thing.

I have had about 20 web companies offer to convert my website to an online ordering system and I told them no. For one, it would be a lot of additional work and money, but more importantly, our delivery partners brought us a good chunk of business. Not only that, but if we had a website, we'd have to invest extra time, energy and money into promoting it, and we were running short on all three.

If your business's primary source of sales is your website, then yes, spend the money and build an awesome website that is super easy to use. Have someone who isn't great at technology check it to make sure it's intuitive and easy to use, because every click a person has to complete costs you 12-20% of sales.

There are a ton of great services now that help you get a website up fast. If you or someone in your network is savvy, WordPress is a great and affordable way to go. If you don't, then try one of the new WYSIWYG (what you see is what you get) web design services like SquareSpace or Wix. These are a little bit more expensive, but they will save you time and energy.

**On your website, be sure to include the following sections:**

- ☐ **About Us:** Your story, mission and background.
- ☐ **Product Descriptions:** Including ingredients, colors, etc. Follow the same steps as your did for digital real estate to make your listings useful and appealing.
- ☐ **Contact Page:** So that people can reach you. Be sure to respond as quickly as possible.
- ☐ **Online Shop:** If you have one, make it easy to find and use.
- ☐ **Social Media and Newsletter Sign-up:** Give people a chance to follow you and stay in touch. Don't over share and periodically reward them for being your friend.

# CREATE EFFECTIVE ADVERTISING

*Effective advertising allows you to reach people who are not searching for your business and to articulate your value quickly and effectively. When done correctly, ads are an affordable way to grow your business.*

Let me tell you a little story about a restaurant called Mosto in Beijing. Every month they ran a small box ad in all of the local expat magazines. It's the cheapest ad there is and most people think it's worthless, but the owners at Mosto knew better.

Back then, I never went to their restaurant because I was poor, but whenever someone asked me which South American restaurant they should go to, it was the only one I could think of. Their strategy had worked!

That is an effective way to advertise in print, but in this digital age it's important to stand out from the noise in whichever way you can. For some businesses, that will be doing online ads, for others, ads in a local coupon book.

For Flower Pepper, we spent our advertising money in two places: we purchased a page in the coupon booklets delivered to your door during our slow months (summers and winters) and also spent a small amount on Facebook advertising in our local area. We chose both of these services because they were geo-targeted: specific to a certain area.

With the coupon book (we used ValPak) we could send coupons to people within a five-mile radius of our restaurant, meaning that our regular customers would get a nice deal, and new customers in the area would be incentivized to pay us a visit.

We then used Facebook to find people who lived or worked in the area, who were likely to eat out (young professionals and college kids) and who were interested in food. Facebook allows you to pick out your ideal audience by age, sex, interests, location, etc., and while the impact wasn't huge, we were able to snag some customers who are really passionate about food and who became our biggest advocates.

Once they liked our Facebook page, we provided them with lots of valuable content, including some recipes, interesting and beautiful videos, and specials announcements that got them excited to come in. We'll talk more about setting up your social media later in this book.

# ELEMENTS OF A GREAT PRINT AD

For a print ad to be effective, it needs to be captivating, clear and conducive to doing business. Always ask yourself: what about this ad will make people spent their money with me? For food, people love a deal. For home services, people love free quotes and price guarantees. For clothing, style and easy returns. For doctors, trust.

**Here are the things you'll want to consider including on your ad:**

- ☐ Pictures of your product
- ☐ Prices of your product, if you are a service people want but don't need or a high-cost item that they will shop around for (like air duct cleaning)
- ☐ Your physical address, plus a map if the location isn't obvious
- ☐ Your contact information: Phone and/or email, plus website
- ☐ Deals that might draw people in
- ☐ If you offer great things on your social media, then social media links.

Here is an example of our Coupons from ValPak. All we had to do was send them the text (they gave us a lot of suggestions on what works best) and they designed it for us.

# ELEMENTS OF A GREAT WEB AD

Web ads are their own beast, and while their effectiveness is a subject of great debate, they are in most cases an easy way to get targeted business and exposure.

That being said, the world wide web is also a cluttered space where everything is competing for clicks and views, so it's critical that you use the right words and the right images to catch your customer's attention.

If you are doing a text only ad (like Google AdWords), start making a list of words and phrases that describe you. Once you've done that, google them and see what other ads come up, and then find a way to differentiate yourself: Better wording? Better deals? Chances are it will be obvious to you once you see their ad. Even if you run a similar ad, AdWords will give you a chance at the first slot by paying more.

For image-based ads on social media, there are a few things that are proven to have great results: pictures of faces draw a lot of attention, as do bright colors. Remember how we talked about tapping into those primal instincts? That's what you're doing here. On Facebook, you can actually do a couple of different designs and check see how they are doing in the back-end.

Another benefit of digital advertising is that you can use it to create custom ads for your different customer bases, meaning that you could have a different ad for the high school students who come in after school and one for their grandmothers who come on Sundays after church, as well as everyone in between.

# WHERE TO ADVERTISE

## Local Newspapers and Magazines

Pricey, but a great way to reach people who still read the paper every day and live in your area. You can request a media kit to learn more about each paper's demographic. When choosing where to print, make sure to choose a paper where your ad won't be drowned out by the competition or seen by the wrong audience.

## College Papers

Affordable but less effective than traditional papers, the benefit of working with college papers is that you can target a very specific area, that you can get great ads designed at reasonable cost, and that the media department will often be able to work with you to do on-campus promotions.

## Coupon Mailers

These have a great ability to put a good deal into the hands of customers in a specific area. It may not seem like a worthwhile investment (you can actually tell, since people have to bring in the coupon), but we found it to be a great way to reach new people. You can also re-use their professional designs to hand out to other customers.

## Facebook

The price depends on how well you create your ad and target it, but it's an affordable, low-investment (you can do a few dollars a day) that allows you to test what works. Facebook has a great dashboard that will show you what ads people clicked on and at what time so you can keep on improving your campaigns.

## Yelp

For restaurants with good reviews, investing in a Yelp campaign can be a great way to get a leg up on the competition by placing your ad over theirs in the search results, and having them not appear in yours. Remember to treat your customers like kings when running these ads, as they tend to attract opinionated people who love writing online reviews.

## Google AdWords

A great and affordable way for brands to secure the number one spot in a Google search, but only if you do it right. Remember to check out what the competition is doing and out do them!

## Groupons

Pricey, since Groupon takes a big chunk of the money, but an effective way to get more exposure in your line of service. Remember to provide great service, since this also tends to attract web-savvy, opinionated people.

For tips and step-by-step tutorials, join our Facebook group!
**www.facebook.com/SmallBusinessMarketingMadeEasy**

# HOW TO GET FREE-ISH ADVERTISING

There are a number of ways to get cheap or discounted advertising.

Every once in a while you'll run across someone who needs to fill in a blank spot in their publication is looking for a place to review, or is hoping to lure you as a customer and wiling to offer you a freebie to pique your interest. The chances of all of these happening will increase dramatically if you've done a good job setting up your online presence and can make it fast and easy for them to feature you.

You can also ask if the publication would be willing to do a barter agreement. That way, you get more bang for your buck, and can write off both the marketing expense and the product cost from your taxes. I would say that during my advertising days about 50% of the ads in my publications were paid for with barter.

You can also repurpose coupons designed for you by someone you advertised with, post them online or give them or your favorite customers so that they bring new people for a BOGO (buy one, get one free) deal.

Since our location was so hidden, I discovered that doing BOGO deals and asking our regulars to bring a friend worked like a charm. One by one, their infectious enthusiasm spread through the community, and not only were we getting new customers, we were also making our existing ones very happy.

Another way I advertised for free was by walking around the neighborhood and handing out posters to other businesses. In them, I offered their employees a 15% discount simply for being close to us. As it turns out, they were thrilled to learn about us, and they also had the same program, so from then on I got discounts on my vitamins, groceries, coffee, pizza, BBQ, wine and ice cream on top of my increased business. Jackpot!

# FREE EDITORIAL WITH ADS

Editorial coverage is non-advertising exposure provided by a newspaper, magazine or website. In some cases, if you buy advertising and ask nicely, your ad rep may be able to send someone over to do a review or interview you for a story.

Whatever you do, though, don't demand that they send someone over. That's tacky, and it could sour the whole relationship. If that happens, editors can place your ads in the worst corners and refuse to publish your special announcements. When I worked as an editor, anyone who demanded I come in automatically got a more critical review because it left me with a sour taste in my mouth. My time was precious, and I hated being told what to do.

Of course, they might also do a review or story if you're not advertising. That's called getting press, and we will talk about that in the next chapter.

# GET THE PRESS YOU DESERVE

*The media is always looking for a great story to tell. If you can share the story of your business and product in an enticing way or help the public solve a problem, then there is free press to be had!*

Press—be it a roundup of local business owners or a review of your business or service—can do wonders things for your business, especially if you are prepared for it. I intentionally left this chapter towards the back because you *must* be ready, if not, you risk harming your business.

When we got our first reviews we were slammed, and at the end of the night we didn't have a single noodle left in the place and spent hours washing up. We survived by a thread, mostly because I am naturally chatty and made sure to regale everyone with tales of our culinary adventures while they waited for their food—an extra marketing opportunity in my eyes, but a potential disaster, for sure.

Many small business owners are so eager to start getting good business that they rush into press and advertising before they have the capacity to handle the crowds that come with it, which can put them in a tough situation: either they make their customers wait, or they compromise their quality. Neither is optimal, though if you need to, making someone wait is always the better option.

Now, there are many different types of free press: television or radio interviews, newspaper, being featured on a popular blog, and more. And it's yours for the taking if you can answer one simple question: How can you make people's lives better or more interesting?

If you are a restaurant, perhaps there is some amazing seasonal recipe or a great origin story that entices people and captures their imagination.

If you sell a product, you might have some really wonderful accessories that are made by a women's cooperative in Sri Lanka, underwear that gives women the butt of a 18-year old, or a children's toy that is proven to boost baby's learning.

If you are a lawyer, a scholar, a coach, a doctor, a finance person or any other service provider, you know that your services are valuable to people, and if you present them in an interesting and timely way, the media will be more than happy to put you out there for their audience.

# GET READY TO TALK TO THE MEDIA

**Make sure your business is ready to go**
If you're not ready to handle the capacity, haven't finished setting up shop or don't have staff to take care of your customers, hold off. You don't want people's first encounter with you to be anything short of amazing, let alone a frazzled mess.

**Determine what to share**
Can you summarize, in one sentence, what it is that will make people stop, watch, listen and focus? Even better, is this something that people will clip, cut and paste, or share on Facebook? This is your golden ticket!

**Prepare your story and materials**
When dealing with the media, it's critical that you are clear and concise. No rambling, no digressions, and no sales pitches. You are giving away a free story or free information in hopes of having people spend their money with you later on: an act of premeditated expectant charity.

**Prepare a sound byte (a brief statement) of each of the items below.**
1. What is your product, and what makes it special?
2. How did you come up with this idea? What makes you an authority on this topic?
3. Who does it serve and what need does it fulfill? What will people get out of it?

**Do your research**
Have a look around. Where do you want to be featured? Is your product suitable for national news or the local news? Who is writing or producing the kinds of articles that feature your type of business? Make a list of publications/shows and the names of the editors and anchors. Then, search their websites to make sure that they didn't just do a piece on what you're proposing.

**Prepare your pitch**
Once you have the list of people you want to talk to, write a custom proposal for each of them, focusing on the benefit to the customer. Put your golden ticket right up front, followed by a brief summary of your background. They will give you one minute at best, so make it count.

**Get in touch with the media**
Finding someone's contact information is pretty easy these days. Usually, you can find their name and a main telephone number in the masthead (list of all staff) of a magazine or newspaper or the "About Us" or "Contact" section on a website. If you can't find their email address online, then call and ask the front desk if they can help you out.

If you are put in touch with the sales department, don't freak out. You don't have to advertise, so just explain to them that you're just now starting and don't have the budget for it yet, but that they will be front of mind if you do. You can definitely invite the sales people or send them samples as a thank you and to get to know more about their products.

# HOW TO ADDRESS YOUR MEDIA PITCH

What I refer to as a media pitch was once referred to as a press release: a short and sweet document that informs the press of what's going on with your business.

Most press releases are blasted to hundreds if not thousands of editors and news producers, and the companies who send them may be able to target specific lists, such as travel agents, North American news media, science writers, etc. If you're a web-based product or service that is doing something seriously newsworthy, then go for this.

If, however, you're a local business or one that's doing something that's already being done, I would take the personal route, and target those people who can get you a ton of good exposure for the same investment you might get from sending a press release into the web.

These people include producers at local TV stations (If you can't find them online, then check sites like LinkedIn), bloggers in your field, newspaper editors, and even people who have mailing lists that provide suggestions for their customers, such as realtors, small business association employees, and more. One of our local realtor friends in Boulder was actually a great source of business.

When writing to these people, be sure to address the letter to them. Letters addressed to "Dear Editor" or even worse "To Whom It May Concern" don't inspire joy in their recipients.

You can even give them a call or shoot them an email in advance and give them a quick heads up that you'd like to send them some information.

Regardless of who you contact them and how, be mindful of their time. They are often bombarded with these kinds of requests, so if you blather on or bore them they might ignore you later. I know that back in the day I would have.

# WHAT GOES INTO A MEDIA PITCH?

There are a number of things all media pitches require: a fantastic, newsworthy headline, a concise summary, the reason why anyone should care, additional information and photos, and your personal contact information.

**The Title**

As briefly as possible, explain why you are newsworthy. If you are having trouble with this, go to the library and read the cover of magazines. Then flip through and read the headlines and the advertising. All of these have mastered the art of the single phrase sales pitch.

**Here are some examples:**
- Local accountant shares 5 unusual tips for saving on your taxes
- New brand releases all natural insert repellant that smells like popsicles
- Italian chef shares 6 amazing cocktails using tomatoes
- Masseuse shares 3 acupressure points that help you lose weight

**The Body**

Give a brief summary of what you've just promised them. Be complete without being verbose. The editor/producer/blogger wants to make sure you're not going to sell them 1 great and 3 lame tips when you've promised 4 great ones.

Quickly explain why their audience would love this. This shows them why it's worth their while, but also that you have done your research and understand what they do.

Afterwards, give them a quick summary of who you are and what you do, qualifying why they should trust you as an authority.

Tell them what's attached. A photo of the person, the dishes or products described, etc. Since your photos are clearly labeled from chapter one I know we don't have to do that now. If your photos are very large, include a resized version and a direct link to download the original photo. You can also link to the complete menu, list of offerings, etc. that we prepared in chapter 1. They will probably ask for it anyways, and now you can provide it to them without feeling rushed.

Once that's done, inform them how you would like to offer your services, whether it's an on-air interview, as a source if they need someone, or as a guest writer. You can also state that you're happy to provide free samples to their staff or gifts as giveaways.

And finally, give them your contact info. All of it. Phone and email, and chat application if that might be useful, website, location address and phone number for your shop, etc.

*HINT: Read through your document. Every single phrase should answer the question: why should they care? If it doesn't, you need more editing.*

# WHY PRODUCERS ARE IGNORING YOU

Ok, so you went through all of that hard work, and nothing. Bad reviews aside, there is no worse feeling in the world. Here's what might have gone wrong:

**They never got it.** Spam happens. Flooded email boxes happen. If you don't hear back, follow up after 2 weeks, and a third time via phone after a month.

**They were busy.** Keep in mind that these people are being bombarded with info and are judged on their ability to pick the cream of the crop. Maybe you didn't fall into that category. If you suspect that might be what's going on, try to catch the smaller fish, whether it's a junior editor, a local paper, or a smaller or local website.

**You didn't write it well.** It happens, which is why I wrote this chapter. Go back and re-read what you've written. I always read things back to myself in a British accent, which helps me detach from my writing and catch anything that is too wordy or clumsy.

**They didn't like your product.** Maybe they aren't into your type of product or don't see the value of your service. Maybe your brand reminded them of something they dislike or maybe you share a name with their ex. Go back, review your offer, and if it still seems great to you, move on to someone else or try another person at the company.

**You didn't offer anything of value.** You think your idea is great, or your $50 giveaway was generous. Maybe they didn't agree. Reconsider what you're offering and try again.

**You pitched at the wrong time.** People in the media need anywhere from one to six months of lead-time for a story, less if it's local TV or radio, of course. If you write too late, then they can't use your summer products until next year, and you won't be new anymore.

Now, I will say, that back when I was an editor I was inundated with these kinds of letters, and I would most commonly turn them down for a) not providing anything novel and b) not explaining it clearly enough. Good pictures always got extra attention, since I needed them to fill my pages and draw the viewers' eyes, as did one-off events, unique expert knowledge, and truly revolutionary things, like a world famous chef setting up shop in town, someone inventing a really cool product, or someone making a really meaningful contribution to society.

**NOTE:** Traditionally, press releases were sent out as files, and contact information was always placed at the top. Since your format will most likely be email, feel free to put your contact information at the bottom. If you're trying to land in a listings magazine, I guarantee the editor will be thrilled if you put your contact information in their format. That way you can just copy and paste it when they publish your product, event or venue information.

# HOW TO BE MORE LIKEABLE

You've landed a media opportunity. Now what?

I feel like this chapter could really appear in half of the chapters of this book, but I placed it here because this is when it really counts. If you go on TV, are interviewed for an article, or have any other exposure to the public and you're not likeable, you've just shot yourself in the foot.

*There are several elements to likeability: confidence, generosity, eloquence, honesty, and great body language.*

**Confidence:** Clearly, anybody who is going to give you their money wants to make sure they are getting what they paid for. Nobody wants to invest in someone who is unsure of themselves, so be sure to rehearse your sound bytes, your confident body language (google Amy Cuddy's "Power Poses"), and to make eye contact with your host and the audience.

**Generosity:** The outlet where you're appearing has just given you a piece of their digital real estate, and the audience a chunk of their time. Now is the time for you to pay them back by giving, giving, giving, and sharing what it is that you have to offer.

**Eloquence:** Sometimes, eloquence means the ability to go on and on and not sound stupid. In this case, it means to sound crisp and sharp in every statement you make. Remember to prepare an outline of sound bytes and rehearse them as much as you can. That way, once you open your mouth nothing but sheer genius will spill from your lips.

**Honesty:** People can spot a liar, so don't say anything that isn't at least 80% true. Some stories are better when embellished and that's fine, but you want to make sure that everything you say is sincere. When you tell lies, your body language changes, and while the audience won't necessarily perceive it as "oh, they are lying!" it might make them feel slightly uneasy, defeating the purpose of going out and trying to make a great impression.

**Body Language:** They say that 80% of what people hear is actually conveyed by your body language. We've already talked about being confident, but make sure that you're open and attentive as well. Look at people's faces, turn towards them, nod in agreement, and allow them to finish speaking. This will make you seem confident, collected, and most importantly: trustworthy.

# DEALING WITH BAD PRESS

Bad press happens, whether it's a negative review or you saying the wrong thing on air. This is the downside to press. While it can be incredibly beneficial, it can also put a ding into your reputation.

You know how they say that there is no such thing as bad press? Hopefully, since you were prepared and generally treat your customers with respect and provide them a great product and service, this is true. But even when it does happen, having good reviews, good marketing and good word of mouth in place can act as a shield to protect you.

In one of the reviews of our restaurant, the critic had mentioned that some of the dishes were not up to snuff. Fortunately, our brand was solid, and that also came through in the review, leading many more people to come in and try us. Some out of curiosity, and some to prove the reviewer wrong. If your brand and your service is good, you'll often get a much milder sentence if your quality slips on the wrong day.

And what's more, unfavorable reviews are usually less memorable than great ones. When people read a good review they make a note to go there. When they read something that is less than great, they might never even commit that to memory. They simply won't make it a point to seek you out, meaning you can still loop them with one of your other marketing methods.

The deciding factor in this situation is the ratio of positive to negative reviews. If you are mostly positive, people will always write off the bad ones as a fluke or a whackadoodle. If you have mostly bad ones, then it's time to seriously reconsider how you're doing business.

# OTHER GREAT WAYS TO GET FREE PRESS

**HARO**

Help a Reporter Out is a free website where daily blasts are sent from reporters requesting expert interviews. They also have a paid service that helps you advertise your products, and the reviews of that service have been quite favorable.

**Donate Raffle Tickets to Fundraisers**

Many big fundraisers will purchase full-page or half-page ads in newspapers to show off their amazing prizes, and if you make a generous enough gift (keeping in mind that it's often deductible, and costs you a lot less than your customer anyways), you can get your logo on the printed materials, as well as some coverage in related articles.

**Submit your contact information to the pubic radio Rolodex**

Many public radio stations have a list of people who are willing to speak on certain topics. Again, even if it's not about your business, they will mention your business when they introduce you.

**Call in to radio shows, comment on forums, etc.**

Ok, so this technically isn't press. But let's imagine you're reading a forum on baby colic, and a person gives fantastic advice. In their signature it says they are the founder of ColicCure. No links, so sales pitch, just the fact that you are part of that company. If you've provided the reader with a great answer to their problem, they will definitely give you a search to find out more about this expert who can solve their problems.

**Put yourself in the Limelight, but not for your business**

If you have the time, volunteer to help with a prominent organization that is often in the press, or develop expertise on a topic. When you are interviewed for your work, they will often refer to you as Mr. or Ms. So-and-So, who does this job and volunteers for this organization. It's not a lot, but it's a great way to nab people who are not in your network.

# TAKE YOUR BRAND TO THE STREETS

*Face-to-face interactions with your customers are an amazing way to form lasting impressions and strong bonds and to get honest feedback on your brand. Studies have shown that physical interaction creates lasting brand impressions.*

Depending on the kind of business you own, going out and interacting with customers may be most of what you do or a special occasion. Regardless of which it is, it serves a unique way to connect with people and leave a lasting impression.

Many small businesses spend tons of money hiring people to do their websites, their social media, and their PR. While all of these things are important, they also have two downsides: both tend to be impersonal, and, unless you are doing an amazingly good job, fall on distracted eyes in an already over-crowded marketplace.

Taking your brand to the street has many benefits. For brick and mortar businesses, you can target people who are in your area, rather than throwing your money at a newspaper ad all across town. You can also distinguish yourself from the competition and introduce people to a product they never knew they needed.

Maybe there are five pizza shops in your area, but yours has a really chewy crust, not to mention an awesome owner with a wicked sense of humor. Or perhaps the customer never knew they would love a linen spray, until they smelled how delightful yours is.

Moreover, human contact such as sampling, eye contact, and physical touch stimulate an area in our brain called the vagus nerve, which is linked to the brain's compassion centers and releases oxytocin, the hormone that creates trust. It is no secret that people have used sampling to sell ages for the past 100 years, and the science says that you should definitely follow suit.

# GREAT PLACES TO CONNECT WITH CUSTOMERS

### Fairs and Farmers Markets
Local fairs, farmer's markets and similar events are a great place to meet people who are prepared to experience new things and spend their money on them. This is more useful for brick and mortar businesses than it is online business, but both can benefit from the exposure, especially if you come prepared. To find these types of events, do a search to see what happened last year, then go and find their main offices and see if you can sign up. If you've missed the deadline, ask them if there is a place you could put some fliers or hand out samples, and if they have a wait list.

### University Events
University students are a curious and hungry bunch, and while they aren't the best customers for all businesses, restaurants, bars, cool crafts, rental cars, etc. can hook a lifetime customer by showing up to these events (which are often quite inexpensive).

### Neighboring Shops, Community Centers, etc.
Some local shops have bulletin boards or small tables where you can leave some business cards or coupons, a great way to reach people who are already shopping in that area. Even if they don't, you can print a poster announcing a neighborhood discount for nearby businesses. We offered people 18% off, got great word of mouth, and actually got discounts in return. Lucky for us, we were next to a bakery, an ice cream shop and a wine shop.

### Events and Workshops
Many entrepreneurs offer workshops online to attract more customers, but even if you're brick and mortar workshops are a wonderful way to meet customers and give them a great impression. We joined a number of events, and people were always interested to hear about what we do, but the real winners were the events we hosted: dumpling classes, exclusive hot pot dinners, and so on. To this day people still email out of the blue, saying they heard about it from a friend and are dying to join one. We organized ours through the local international group on Meetup.com.

### Outside of your Shop
You're going to meet a ton of customers inside of your shop, but what about people near your shop? I spent a day visiting all the nearby offices and giving them our takeout menu. It was a great chance to get face time with them and to share our story. I had also planned on delivering menus to nearby homes and schools, but business was so good I didn't have to.

### Tradeshows
Depending on your time and resources, trade shows can be a great way to connect with a national and international audience, though they require a lot of startup cost. Be sure to thoroughly vet the event and do a cost benefit analysis before taking the plunge.

# DOING A NEIGHBORHOOD DISCOUNT

As said, doing a neighborhood discount is a great way to connect with people who live and work in your neighborhood.

Back when we opened, I made an 11x17 poster that was fun, represented who we were as a brand and offered a discount, and then I went to every nearby shop in the afternoon (when things are slow) and asked if I could hang it in their break room. We got a ton of great regulars, and when some local shoppers overheard my request they immediately came over to check out the new place that had opened across the street.

你好！你吃饭了吗？

## Have you eaten?

"Have you eaten?" is how Chinese people greet one another, and it's how we wanted to introduce ourselves to you.

We just moved in across the street (next to Boulder Valley Credit Union) and would love to invite you to have lunch with us.

Just let us know you're from the neighborhood shops and we'll give you 15% off your lunch bill.

Our mission at Flower Pepper is to serve up authentic Chinese home cooking. Nothing fried, nothing sticky, and no brown sauce.

Flower Pepper Restaurant
Authentic Chinese Home Cooking

Call ahead! (720) 381-1594
2655 Broadway • flowerpeppereats.com

# WHAT TO PREPARE FOR EVENTS

When you're getting ready to join an event, you want to make sure that you have some product for your new customers to experience, your sound bytes down pat, and your printed collateral so that they can find you later. Small gifts are always welcome (especially if they are branded), but not necessary.

Before you start preparing, ask yourself what you want to get out of this event. Do you want more exposure? Do you want to build a mailing list? Do you want to sell something at the event?

The next question you need to ask yourself is what people at this event would actually like to have. Students want free samples and snacks, especially around lunch time, but someone at a farmers' market may want to buy something or get your information for later (if they've just arrived). At professional fairs, people often like to grab some really fun and useful swag. I would always ask myself if it's something my office manager Liz would go downstairs to grab one of.

Whatever you decide to do, be sure to bring business cards, menus or fliers, and lots of them. All of your printed materials should include the best things about your business (your selling points) as well as all of your contact information: web, phone, address (if brick and mortar) and web address.

If you are a service provider, make sure that you include a list of services, rather than just a business card. The person who sees your flier may not need a lawyer now, for instance, but if you list your services they are more likely to think of you when they do.

# How to Host an Event

Our competition had a monthly "Lucky Dinner" where a dozen people were invited to dine with her, but she only announced it on her website, so it never really took off as a big event.

We decided to go the opposite route, find people who were interested in what we do, and offer them an event.

We used Meetup.com to connect with some local groups, and talked to the admin of the international and food groups to see if they'd like to host an event with us. They were thrilled! We did a combination of events, including a class on making dumplings, *zongzi* (sticky rice filled banana leaves) and a few hot pot dinners. Each one of these events was booked solid with people who had never heard of us, and became a great tool to create word of mouth buzz.

While it's tempting to do a free event (and may be appropriate, depending on what you do) we actually charged 10-25 dollars for each event, and people were happy to pay it. We had waitlists for each event, and people were always pressing us to host more.

**Here are some simple suggestions to help you plan an amazing event:**

- **Pick an interesting topic related to your business.** It may be a hike on which you introduce your gear (rather than an in-store presentation), a class on how to dress for success using your line of clothes, or a cupcake decorating class.

- **Pick your audience.** For us, Meetup.com was great, but if you're in a professional field, you may want to reach our to professional organizations such as the local small business association, networking groups, etc. Facebook also has good groups, and you can find a ton of stuff online by googling your area of interest and your geographical region.

- **Think through the experience.** You're the expert, so you want to come prepared. Do you need handouts? Photos? Samples? Extra plates? Do you want to offer people a coupon? Have them sign up for your list?

  Write out all the possibilities and plan for them.

- **Come prepared.** Show up early to set up so that you're not stressed when it starts.

- **Mingle and follow up.** Take some time afterwards to chat with people and get to know them. If people gave you their contact information, be sure to follow up, tell them how much you enjoyed meeting them, and offer them something useful. Don't try to sell your product, but instead, offer them another useful morsel. The business will come soon enough.

# Grow your Relationships On Social Media

*Social Media allows you to share your brand story with people around the world, but more importantly, with your customers. By building a great relationship and offering value, you can stand out in a sea of social posts and stay front-of-mind at all times.*

People treat social media like it's the holy grail of marketing. For some companies it is, but for small businesses, mom and pop shops and brick and mortar establishments, other ways of marketing are far more effective, which is why we've put this off until now. Allow me to explain.

Social media is a beautiful mess of people's updates, interesting articles, late breaking news, ads and cat videos. It is fascinating but cluttered, and the exposure that you get there is going to be minimal, since you're always going to be competing with a number of other posts. If you're a huge company that has a big budget to make viral videos, then yes, social media is going to be a game changer. If you're a renowned brand that people seek out for information and cool content, then social media is *the* place to connect with customers. If, however, you are a small business, you might not have the budget to create viral content or daily updates that are newsworthy.

So do you have to do social media at all? The short and definitive answer is yes. Here's why: When done right, it's a great way to connect with people outside of your network. It's a great place to tell your company story, so that when people go and find you online, they get a sense of who you are and begin to build trust in you and your brand.

People can also use it to reach out to you to ask questions, and with young people, doing so on social media is often more intuitive than doing it via phone or email.

Furthermore, it's a great way to increase your chances of being found online, especially if your name isn't 100% unique. If you only have a website, then you might be further down on the rankings, but social media profiles are much more easily found.

# THINGS THAT WORK ON SOCIAL MEDIA

**Moving Images**
Things that move immediately draw the eye and create intrigue. If done well, videos, gifs and vines will help draw the customer in because our inner monkey cannot resist movement. Make sure that what you're drawing them into is worth watching though, or else they might not stick around, or worse, they might block you.

**Bright Colors and Faces**
Social media is often dubbed "anti-social media" but at its core, it's still all about the things that attract us in real life: smiling faces, sexy images, bright colors and action. We are all human, after all. When picking your colors, be sure to pick something that will stand out against the platform's design. Let's say you're trying to sell a shirt. Advertising the one that is Facebook blue on Facebook might make it get lost in the crowd.

**Touching, Inspiring or Terrifying Stories**
People these days have less and less social contact, but we still crave the emotional rush that comes from seeing something moving, something scary or something inspiring. If you can make people feel something, they will share your content, and that is the holy grail of business marketing.

**Funny Clips or Memes**
Just as people want to feel something, people also want to be amused. Most people who are on social media are there because they are avoiding the boring mundacity of their life. Make them laugh and they will thank you for it with their business

**Food**
Some research has shown that women think about food as much as men think about sex, which is about every half hour. We love food, and if you can share something that is both mouth-watering and novel, you're bound to grab people's attention.

**Freebies**
People cannot resist a freebie, but keep in mind that you are competing with the whole of the Internet. Make sure your freebie is interesting and rewarding enough for your customers to give you a few minutes out of their busy schedules.

**Being Useful**
Everyone has problems. If you're in the business of solving problems, why not give away some free advice to grow your following. You could do a Q&A, share some of your cooking secrets, or demonstrate a novel way to use your product (like showing off how to dress up and down the shoes you sell, or how to decorate around your product).

# HOW TO STRUCTURE A SOCIAL MEDIA POST

How you style your social media content is as important as the actual content itself. That's why in recent years SMO, or Social Media Optimization, has become a must-have skill for all social media marketers. In short, SMO is the creation of shareable content, and placing it in the right places.

**User-Friendly Content**

Your content will vary greatly depending on whom you are writing it for, but one thing is key: you must hook your audience. Always create a headline and first sentence that grabs people's attention in the first 20 words.

**Tag People and Places**

The point of social media content is to be shared, and one great way to alert people to your stuff by tagging them! When you do, they will automatically get a notification, and if your content is truly shareable, they will start spreading it to their networks as well. Even if the content doesn't get shared, you tagging them will cause your content to show up on their timeline, where everyone in their network can see this.

Very early on, my husband did a post about the woman who owned a nearby BBQ shop and tagged her in it. Everyone loved seeing small businesses supporting one another, and it gave both of our establishments a boost in business.

**Turn on your Locations**

While it's a good idea to turn off locations on private posts (you don't want obsessed noodle fans stalking you!) turning on the location on business posts is actually a great way for people who are checking out the neighborhood to find you. This is a great compliment to your digital real estate.

**Tag Yourself**

When you first set up your social media accounts it will be slow. We'll talk about how to jumpstart that in the next pages, but in the meanwhile, feel free to tag yourself! This will cause your page to show up on your personal feed and will create some intrigue amongst your family and friends.

**Use Hashtags**

When posting to Twitter and Instagram, using the right hashtags (keywords with the # sign placed in front of them) will allow people who are interested in your content to easily find you when they do a search. #locally owned #small business #restaurant #boulderco were all good ones for us.

# Jumpstart your Social Media Following

There is nothing more depressing than setting up a social media account and not getting good results. Much like web traffic and foot traffic, a social media following takes time to build, but fortunately there are a few things you can do to jumpstart it.

### Tag Everyone
Your friends, your family, complete strangers... Once you have some solid content up online (no one will like an empty profile) spend some time to ask people in your network to like the page, tag people who will like it, or write on relevant people's or businesses walls and let them know that you are around and worthy of a like or follow.

### Follow Others
Another easy way to get people to like and follow you is to like and follow them. When you do so, they receive an announcement and will likely click on your profile to see who you are, and if your profile and content is enticing, they might just like you back.

### Build Lists
Twitter has a neat function that allows you to build lists of people and name them. If Twitter is one of the platforms you choose (more on that in the next chapter) this is a great way to get someone's attention. I remember the day someone added me to a list called "Awesome Writers" and to this day I follow that person like a hawk. When you make others feel important they will repay you in kind.

### Advertise
Advertising is a great way to get followers who are interested in your product. Facebook allows you to determine the goal of your ads (everything from likes to clicks to followers), and you can hone in on their age, interests, gender and location. Both the price and the results will fluctuate on a number of factors, so play around with it to see what works best for you and your business.

The more likes you have the more likeable you become (people will be more attracted to your profile since you have social validation, and the sites will rank you higher as you provide better quality), so you can consider doing a mixed strategy of penny likes (google it!) and targeted advertising.

### Don't Buy Followers
There are a number of companies that will provide you with a hundred to a thousand followers for a lump sum, but they aren't always legit and can trigger the website to block your accounts, since purchasing followers and likes violates the terms of service. Better to do it the honest way.

# DIFFERENT SOCIAL MEDIA OUTLETS

**Facebook**
This universal platform is good for building a strong following no matter what business you're in, since it allows you to share content in a number of ways. Start by asking your friends and family to follow you, then run a small ad campaign to loop in other people.

**Twitter**
Better for educators (coaches, writers, etc.) who can loop people into a conversation by posting interesting things. A great tool for conversations.

**Google Plus**
While Google Plus has great search engine optimization, it's best used for sharing within certain demographics and professional networks. Optimal for most small businesses.

**Pinterest**
Pinterest is extremely popular with women and a great way to share products and information that are useful or beautiful. It has very good searchability and is a great platform for being found if you describe things well. Think of it as putting your things into one great big library.

**Instagram**
Instagram, commonly referred to as IG, is a great place to share your stunning photos, though it's not as searchable as Pinterest. If your product is something that can be seen in action (clothes, hairstyles, creative foods, travel, etc.) this is a great channel to show off your work.

**LinkedIn**
Good for professionals who have business-related ideas to share. I also recommend creating a profile for yourself and filing out the company's profile in great detail, since that will increase the chances of people finding you online.

**Specialty Forums**
There are endless websites and specialty forums for everything from gluten-free baking to fertility. Spend some time on these forums answering people's questions, and link to your website in your signature. Don't promote your product. Let them come to you naturally.

**Snapchat**
A great place to meet young people and to share your company's story with them. If you are pressed for time and your audience is not between 16-26, I'd recommend skipping this. If they are, however, and you do have time, this is a wonderful way to share insight into your business.

**HINT:** For all of these platforms, be sure to check in once a day to see if anyone is trying to reach you. Angry customers will reach out on social media and handling the situation quickly you can make them happy and avoid any further bad press.

# MARKETING NEWSLETTERS

Do a search for "list building" and you'll find dozens of companies, courses and coaches telling you that you must create a mailing list for your business.

While I don't think it's a complete necessity, having access to your customers can be a great benefit to your business because it allows you to reach people directly. On the other hand, it can also be a detriment if you send them junk they don't need or want.

If you think that you can provide your customers with good content, then create a mailing list with MailChimp, AWeber, Constant Contact or a similar site. You can then offer a coupon, free sample with purchase or an eBook to those who sign up to establish yourself as an expert or promote your products.

What you don't want to do is add people to the mailing list without their permission. Email newsletters are also called "permission marketing" because the customers have given you expressed permission to contact them, often via a double sign-in process where they have to confirm that they signed up for the newsletter by clicking a link.

Like social media, a good newsletter starts with a great headline. Offer something useful, something impressive, or simply a discount to celebrate whatever occasion.

Most newsletter software have a control panel where you can see how many people opened your newsletter, how long they read it for and how many people unsubscribed. This is a great way to learn more about your audience's likes and dislikes and hone to your overall marketing strategy.

**HINT:** In most software you can do A/B testing to determine what customers want. So if you can't decide which title is better, send one title to half of your list and one title to the other half, then see what happens.

# KEEPING TRACK OF RESULTS

Now, the thing about marketing is that it's hard to tell what the results are from a campaign were, especially if you're running more than one at a time. On social media and with newsletters, you can see how much people are engaging with your content, which is a great way to hone in on your customer's likes and dislikes, as well as that fuzzy gray area in between where they just don't care.

Often times these tools are called "analytics" or "dashboard" and there you can find how many people viewed your content, clicked on it, shared it, etc., as well as how many people unfollowed you. Personally, I think those are the key elements you need to analyze, even though there is a plethora of other information.

To keep track of all of this, you can set up an Excel sheet or a notebook where you create a chart like this:

| Date | Campaign | Platform | Likes | Shares | Follows | UnFollows | Notes |
|------|----------|----------|-------|--------|---------|-----------|-------|
|      |          |          |       |        |         |           |       |
|      |          |          |       |        |         |           |       |
|      |          |          |       |        |         |           |       |

You can also have a column for each platform, such as: Facebook Likes, Pins, Newsletter Subscribers…

Here you can keep track of people's responses to your content. It's as simple as that. If you're an Excel junkie like me, you'll also write in a formula that calculates % growth, although for most small businesses you'll be able to see what's happening by just glancing at the columns.

In Notes, you can keep track of your thoughts. People love donuts and puppies, don't like coffee posts at night, prefer women over men in ads, etc.

**Some trends you want to look out for are:**
- Are people responding to this type of content?
- Is there a certain day or a certain time of day that people like to receive my content?
- Do people like this type of headline or that type of headline?
- What makes people like me? What makes people purchase from me?
- What ads to people purchase from?

# WEAVE YOURSELF A PROFIT NETWORK

*Networking with other business owners, professional organizations and groups of customers creates a steady stream of income, word of mouth buzz, and ongoing opportunities to promote your business.*

In the past few chapters we've discussed marketing to the individual customer. When I was sharing the idea for this book with my friend Chelsey, she pointed out that networking should be its own chapter.

As a seasoned marketing consultant she has found that networking is one of the most powerful tools business owners can employ to create more opportunities for sales, promotions and word of mouth buzz, even if the people you network with aren't your direct customers.

There are two ways of creating profit networks. One is networking with people one on one at events, and the other is selling to businesses. In the first scenario, you spread the word about your business to people who know people outside of your network, so that they can expand your reach. In the second scenario, you reach out to the person who is in charge of making the decision to purchase your product (often the office manager or HR manager) and see if there is an opportunity to serve their company.

# HOW TO SELL TO BUSINESSES

For some of you, B2B (business to business) may be your primary source of sales, but if your sales are primarily B2C (business to consumer) there are some great opportunities to cater to bigger clients, locking in large-volume sales.

To do this, start by brainstorming a list of companies who may need your services. If you are a restaurant, this would be companies nearby or those who are likely to cater events (if you do this). If you're a print shop, then you'll want to talk to wedding planners, offices with public outreach, and conferences. You get the gist.

Once you have a list of businesses, go online and try to figure out which person you need to talk to. You can often find the right person on the website, LinkedIn, or simply by calling the receptionist and asking.

For each company, but together a small package that has a letter explaining how you can serve them, and any relevant marketing materials, such as menus, a one-sheet with recommended products, etc.

Now, some people recommend calling before sending the package. I like to send it, and call before it has arrived. Why? Because if you ask for permission to send it they might say no, and if you call them afterwards they might have already tossed it.

I personally pop it in the mail, then give them a call and say: "Hi So-and-So! I just sent you a letter because I think I could serve you or your customers well. I know you're busy and you might not need it now, but have a look, and call me if you want to cooperate, or save it for later. All of my information is included in the package."

Now I have created intrigue, shown that I care about the customer and make a personal impression. When the person receives the package they are more likely to give it a closer look. I've also subconsciously seeded the idea that they may want to hang on to the package until they need it.

# HOW NETWORKING EVENTS WORK

You attend a meeting of the Small Business Association, Toastmasters, or other professional networking group, armed with your elevator pitch, your sound bytes, and your business card. At this event, you meet 50 people, and have meaningful conversations with 10 of them. Most of them are in different lines of work, have a different customers base, and may not need your services now. Once you get home, you'll email them, follow them on LinkedIn, and maybe even add them on Facebook, and make it a point to keep in touch even if they aren't bringing you business.

At this point you're probably thinking: "Why the heck am I going to this meeting then?!"

You are going to this meeting because you are seeding word of mouth agents who have met you, like you, and who have their own networks of trusting friends and family, a.k.a.: your future customers. They may not need your services now, or ever for that matter, but when they or their contacts do, you will be the first person to pop into their minds because you've made such a great impression.

They might even go above and beyond and promote you to their network, which is especially useful if you provide services, like graphic design or accounting. These are the kinds of people that everyone needs, but nobody has the time or experience to evaluate thoroughly.

Let's do a conservative estimate. You go to an event and click with ten people. Those people all have a network of 100 friends and customers. That's 1,000 potential customers, plus *their* friends and family. And remember, that's a conservative estimate, and the sky is the limit if you come prepared.

They are right when they say that the "fortune is in the follow-up." So go, connect, stay connected, and be top of mind for them when they need you.

# HOW TO PREPARE FOR A NETWORKING MEETING

A lot of this book will have prepared you for coming to a networking meeting. You know your elevator pitch, you have business cards, and you have great material to follow up with. You see! There was a method to my madness all along. By helping you create really great, honest and trustworthy materials along the way, you can now reach some of the most effective promoters and lock them in. CLICK!

**So here's what you need to bring:**

- **Business Cards:** These should include your name, business name, contact information for both, and art that gives them a sense of who you are.

- **Printed Materials:** Definitely bring this is you have a booth. If it's for a networking meeting, keep a copy or two in your bag in case anyone is super interested. You can say you took one to give to your neighbor, but are happy to share it with them.

- **Your Elevator Pitch:** Dazzle them in 30 seconds or less!

- **Your Sound Bytes:** Networking events are about networking, so make sure you know these by heart so that you're not wasting anyone's time.

- **Your Curiosity:** Yes, you're going to share what you do, but if you make it a point to listen to your new network, they will remember how nice and attentive you were. Being a good listener who asks good questions makes a *great* impression.

# WHAT IF YOU'RE TOO SHY TO NETWORK?

This is a really common question, and there are a couple of different ways to think about it. If you're an introvert then these events can be really overwhelming. If you're insecure, they are terrifying. And if you are a shy person, it might be hard for you to put yourself out there.

Now, I want you to take a step back and look at yourself. You have set up a business. You have taken on the one challenge that 90% of Americans are too scared to do. If you ask me, you are an unstoppable force, and I know that if you push yourself just a little bit further, you can network with great ease.

Here are some tips that have helped me:

**If you are insecure...**
Go back and look at everything you have accomplished so far. Write a narrative of how your business started, and all of the things you've accomplished, no matter how small, and then write a vision for the next year. This will give you perspective, and coupled with your well-rehearsed sound bytes you'll feel much more confident.

**If you are shy...**
I am both shy and quiet, but I knew that if I wanted to educate people I had to learn to own my own voice. So you know what I did: I started recording fake interviews with myself. It allowed me to go back, evaluate myself (the cringe only lasted a short while), and most importantly, to grow comfortable with a camera being pointed in my face. Once you master that, going face to face with others won't be so terrifying.

**If you are introverted...**
I am very introverted and someone who can spend hours and days just hanging out with her own mind. I do ok in crowds, but I never feel elegant or myself because my brain shuts down after a while. For this, I developed a simple three part strategy: small talk, question, personal connection statement. I introduce myself in the usual way: what do you do, lovely dress, etc. I then focus on asking questions rather than just giving simple responses. Then, I try to find something that binds us together. It can be a joke, a suggested meeting, or even the offer to go grab them a drink. I run this mental checklist as I am going around the room, and it helps me stayed focused and create connection with individuals, rather than being overwhelmed by the flood of people.

# WHAT TO DO AFTER A NETWORKING MEETING

They say the fortune is in the follow-up. They – whoever they are – are correct, especially after a networking meeting.

Unlike your other promotional efforts, networking is about creating a profit network that extends to places you haven't reached yet via the people you're networking with. By forming mutually beneficial relationships with these people you gain instant access to their network, which in turn creates more business for you, even when you're not working.

Not only that, but social contact is good for us. When we do regular marketing, we are talking to strangers, trying to convince them to give us their attention and their money. When we network, we are building relationships with people we like and respect, who in turn help to promote our businesses.

So, once you've met someone you click with at a networking event, you should send a follow-up email. This should include the fact that it was nice to meet them, a brief reference to something you've talked about or a compliment, and the wish to stay in touch. Keep it under 250 words, and don't spent too much time talking about yourself.

Be sure to include all of your information in your email signature so you can spark their memory and make it easy to find you or forward your information to someone who needs your services.

In my case, I would sign my email:

Jennifer Thomé
Co-Founder, Flower Pepper Restaurant – Authentic Chinese Home Cooking
Jennifer@flowerpeppereats.com | 202-670-9888

OR

Jennifer Thomé,
CEO and Strategic Marketing Consultant @ PraMaSo – Practical Marketing Solution
Jennifer@pramaso.com | 202-670-9888

# BE NICE TO YOUR NETWORK

One great way to follow up is to share something, but what should you share?

**Here are some suggestions:**

**Share an Article**
Add a quick note saying that you think they will find this useful or interesting, and that you hope all is well. I sometimes get these from people I've totally forgotten, and it's such a great and subtle reminder that they exist.

**Offer them a Discount**
Offering a discount or a special package is a great way to drive business from nearby organizations, as long as you're not tacky about it.

**Pay a Compliment**
Offering a compliment on their latest media appearance, award, launch, or a product that you recently tried is a great way to keep in touch.

**Purchase their Products**
But first, ask for a recommendation. That way you can have that contact, support them, and forge a deeper relationship.

**Introduce them to Friends**
Whether it's for social reasons or business, everyone appreciates being thought of and connected.

**Just say Hi!**
Owning a small business can be isolating. If you have nothing else to offer ping them with a warm hello and "how are you?"

*HINT! Remember to sign every email with your company signature, so that you can slowly sear your name into their memory.*

# HOW TO DEAL WITH MOOCHERS

Once you start building your reputation you'll find that this world is full of moochers: people who want your products or your expertise but aren't willing to give you anything in return.

I can't count the number of times I've had people ask for free advice, free work and free samples. In some situations, they have gone so far as to ask for proposals and to lift the ideas and assign them to an intern. That stung, but I know from experience that it happens every day and that it wasn't personal.

**Here a few clever ways that you can handle the moochers:**

**Set a Consultation Fee**
If you suspect someone is trying to steal too much of your time, tell them that this question is too complex to be handled in this way and offer a consultation. This can be at a reduced rate, but be sure to convey that you're a pro and that you value your time.

**Set some Rules**
When you get clear on what you will and won't give away, it's easy to tell people that your company policy is not to donate lunches, samples, or services unless it's for a nonprofit or media opportunity. You can then offer them a discount instead, if you are so inclined.

**Keep a Library or Blog**
When someone asks you a question, you can refer them to an article, preferably one you wrote. If you have a mailing list, you can also ask them to sign up there since you offer great advice for free all the time.

**Set a Discount**
I'm all about supporting other organizations and I know that sometimes things get tight, but I'm not about giving away things for free. When needed, I have a set discount I apply to organizations that deserve it.

**The Exceptions**
For every rule there is an exception. In this case, there are two: media opportunities and nonprofits. The former will help you accelerate your business, but be savvy and choose the right one. The latter can make your soul sing and reduce your tax burden.

*My rule of thumb is this: if the answer cannot be explained in 250 words or 5 minutes, then it's time to charge a consultation fee.*

# TYPES OF NETWORKING EVENTS

If you're feeling stuck as to what kind of event you should attend, here is a list to get you started.

**Small Business Organizations**
Network with groups of likeminded people while also honing your skills as a business owner.

**Special Interest Networking Organizations (for women, people of a certain profession, etc.)**
No better way to target your key demographic and meet go-getters in their field.

**Local Fairs**
A fantastic place to meet people who are located in your city and who are out with the specific motive go find new businesses to support.

**Toastmasters and other Skills-Based Courses**
Like networking organizations, these are full of people who have the money to seek out self-improvement and who tend to be engaged connectors.

**Charity Events or Nonprofit Volunteer Experiences**
Here you can support causes that you love, and meet people who you have two things in common with: passion and a dedication to improving the world through service.

**Trade Shows**
At trade shows it's harder to make solid contacts, but they are still a great place to get to know companies that offer mutual benefit. You can always search out the owner of companies you admire, that are useful or nearby afterwards.

**Lectures with Receptions**
Universities and professional organizations offer speaker series on any subject imaginable, and are a great place to learn, be stimulated, and meet like-minded people.

# PUTTING IT ALL TOGETHER

I often am asked for a specific day-by-day marketing plan that will help a small business double or triple their revenue. Well, if I had that plan I would be a millionaire, because the very nature of small business – serving a unique set of customers using your best talents – means that there are thousands of potential marketing plans out there, and it's up to your to create, refine and deploy one that's right for you.

Much of it will be trial and error, and as I've mentioned throughout this book, when you start by setting up your digital real estate and maintaining it, you'll always have a solid foundation to stand on while you reach for the stars with your marketing efforts.

The way I went about my marketing plan was to do one thing every day. Why? Because that's all I could handle!

This allowed me to move forward without panicking, getting overwhelmed or growing resentful of the business.

On some days, this meant a social media post, on others, responding to reviews online. Sometimes it meant taking an hour to update the website, and when I was feeling generous with myself, it meant talking off the customer's ears while they were waiting for their take out order.

What I like to do now is to do a mental dump of all the marketing ideas I have on a piece of paper, decide which ones I'd like to try first, and then put them into my calendar for that month.

The calendar I use has 4 columns: the days of the month, my marketing project, my exercise (which can be 5 minutes of yoga or an hour-long run) and my chores, and these categories (marketing aside) change every single month. Being a small business owner means that it's up to you to find balance, and I use this system to remind myself of the areas I need to work on so that I don't feel like my work is ruining my life.

# THE NEVER-ENDING MARKETING STORY

Admit it: there have been times in this book that you've been tempted to just hire a consultant to do your marketing and get it over with.

As a part-time marketing consultant I am not opposed to that, of course, but I have spoken to a lot of entrepreneurs and small business owners who think that it's a one shot deal and done: you do a great marketing campaign or launch a viral video and BAM! You are set for life. Everyone knows you name, and spends the rest of their lives throwing money at your.

Now, if that were the case, why do you think McDonalds and other major chains are still advertising after all these years?

There is always more money to be had, but more importantly, there are always going to be customers to replace. People move, people outgrow your product or find something else they like better, and at the same time, there are always new customers who are ready to find your product. There are 360,000 people born into this world every day, and while it's hard to imagine all of them becoming your customers, there is something really powerful about envisioning your business as one that will continue to flourish and grow.

We never know where our small business journey is going to take us. Perhaps you'll do it for a few years before craving the stability of a desk job, or perhaps you'll go on to franchise your business or start something entirely new. Maybe you'll do this business until the day you retire and pass it on to your kids.

No matter what you decide to do, you are creating your own legacy, a story that will define both you and your business for years to come. That is the very core of marketing – crafting and telling the story of your business and your life as a business owner, and that is a story that is never-ending.

# THE ~~END~~ BEGINNING

Well, this book has come to an end, but your small business marketing journey is only just beginning, and I know that armed with these eight key concepts you'll have no trouble staying in touch with your old customers and finding a steady stream of new ones.

Now there will times when running a business is totally overwhelming and you won't feel like promoting. We've been there. At times we were so busy that we'd be washing dishes until midnight, and have to be back at 5am to prep for the next day. Those days were hard, but because out digital real estate was so well developed, it was doing passive marketing for us even when we couldn't.

During those times, the only thing we'd do was to throw up a post on Facebook warning our regulars that it was crazy and that they should order ahead or go somewhere else. Even though that was the fastest, laziest post I could have written it drove take out business, as our regulars were reminded of how good our food is, and really appreciative that we would take the time to let them know about the long lines.

Hopefully you'll have the same thing happening in your business soon!

After a really great but truly exhausting year, Jeff and I decided that the day-to-day hustle of a popular spot was too much for us and decided to sell. Yes, we are crazy, and yes, as we watched revenue continue to increase month after month there were days that we regretted it, but the six-figure payment the new owners gave us for the business and its reputation helped cushion the blow.

There is no guarantee that you'll be able to get the same results, but small businesses service, succeed and flourish every single day. You know as well as I do, that when you bring quality, passion and resourcefulness to the table, your customers will happily reward you with their love and their loyalty.

Now, I know you're itching to get started, and I am excited to help you on your journey, so I hope that you will stay in touch with me through the Facebook page. There you can ask questions, share your success, and learn about new tools. You can join by visiting this link:
**www.facebook.com/SmallBusinessMarketingMadeEasy**

www.ingramcontent.com/pod-product-compliance
Lightning Source LLC
Chambersburg PA
CBHW050746180526
45159CB00003B/1366